# The Mount Rushmore Presidents

Rosie McCormick

Core Knowledge

Copyright © 2019 Core Knowledge Foundation
www.coreknowledge.org

All Rights Reserved.

Core Knowledge®, Core Knowledge Curriculum Series™,
Core Knowledge History and Geography™, and CKHG™
are trademarks of the Core Knowledge Foundation.

Trademarks and trade names are shown in this book
strictly for illustrative and educational purposes and are
the property of their respective owners. References herein
should not be regarded as affecting the validity of said
trademarks and trade names.

Printed in Canada

ISBN: 978-1-68380-376-8

# The Mount Rushmore Presidents

## Table of Contents

# Four Great Presidents

The president is the leader of the United States. Four of our greatest presidents are honored at Mount Rushmore. Their faces have been carved in stone on this mountainside in the Black Hills of South Dakota. These four men are George Washington, Thomas Jefferson, Theodore Roosevelt, and Abraham Lincoln.

It took over fourteen years to finish carving the faces. Workers blasted huge chunks of rock off the mountain to make four head shapes. The men who carved the stone had to hang from ropes high above the ground.

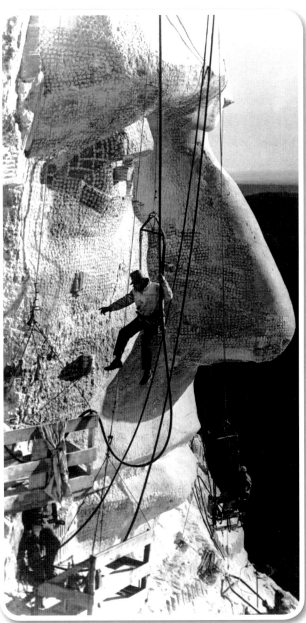

They used special tools to carve the eyes, noses, and mouths. The noses on the faces they carved are taller than a person!

How does a person get to be the president? In the United States, the people elect, or choose, the president. In some countries, people don't get to choose their own leader. You probably have heard about kings and queens.

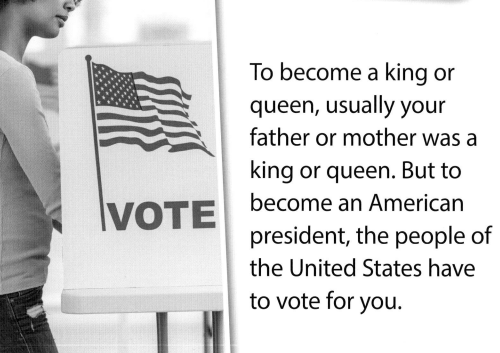

To become a king or queen, usually your father or mother was a king or queen. But to become an American president, the people of the United States have to vote for you.

What kind of person do you think the president should be? Most people would say that the president should be honest, smart, fair, and brave. Who can become president?

Can a farmer become president? Yes—George Washington was once a farmer.

Can an inventor become president? Yes—Thomas Jefferson was an inventor.

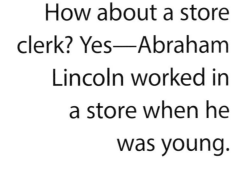

How about a store clerk? Yes—Abraham Lincoln worked in a store when he was young.

And how about a cowboy? Yes—Theodore Roosevelt once worked as a cowboy.

The president of the United States works in our nation's capital, Washington, D.C. He lives and works in a building called the White House. You may have seen the White House on television or in magazines or newspapers. It's very large, with many rooms.

The president helps to run the country. The Oval Office, where the president works, is shaped like an egg.

The White House has its own bowling alley and movie theater. And when presidents travel, they can take a helicopter from the lawn of the White House.

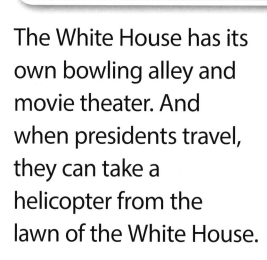

# George Washington

There is a story about George Washington as a young boy. We know the story is not true, but it is a good one to tell anyway.

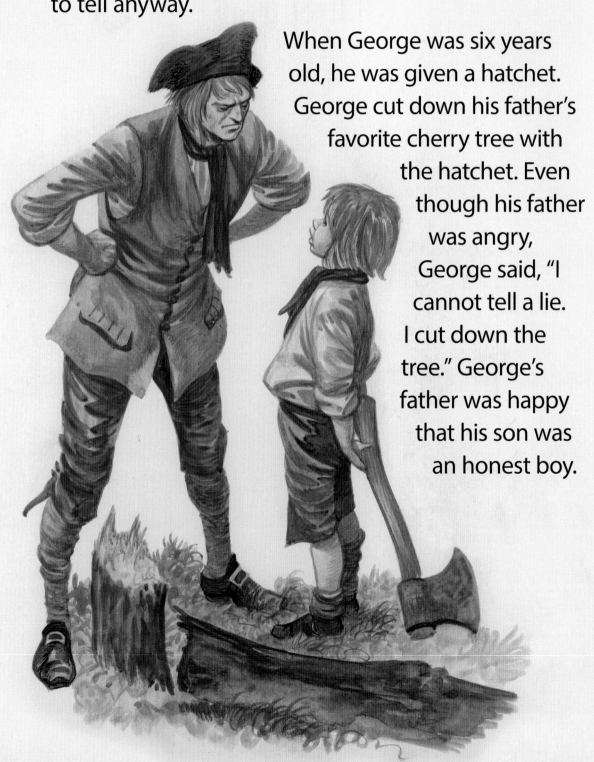

When George was six years old, he was given a hatchet. George cut down his father's favorite cherry tree with the hatchet. Even though his father was angry, George said, "I cannot tell a lie. I cut down the tree." George's father was happy that his son was an honest boy.

When George grew up, he became a surveyor, or a person who measures big pieces of land in order to make maps. George loved doing this job because he could go off exploring. George explored Virginia and bought land there.

When George married, he and his wife, Martha, lived in Virginia. They lived on a large farm named Mount Vernon. Mount Vernon is on the Potomac River and is close to Washington, D.C.

George was chosen to be the leader of the American army. The American army fought the British army.

George was a great leader. The American army beat the British, and the United States became a free nation.

When the United States needed its first president, the people chose George. They knew that he was an honest man, a hard worker, and a good soldier.

Because George Washington was our first president, he is called the "Father of Our Country."

# Thomas Jefferson

Thomas Jefferson was born in Virginia many years before the United States became a country. Thomas had six sisters and three brothers.

The family lived on a large farm. Thomas didn't go to school. A tutor, or teacher, came to his house, and they read together. Many people today visit Thomas's childhood home.

When Thomas was seventeen years old, he went to the College of William and Mary in Virginia. He was a hardworking student.

Thomas learned many languages, including Italian, Spanish, and French. His favorite subject was math. Thomas became a lawyer.

Thomas planned and built a family home in Virginia named Monticello. The word *Monticello* means "little mountain" in Italian. Thomas lived at Monticello with his wife, Martha, and their children.

Today, many people visit Monticello to learn about Thomas's life.

Thomas liked to invent things. He invented a machine that could make two copies of a handwritten letter.

Before Thomas Jefferson became the third president of the United States, he wrote the Declaration of Independence.

This important letter was sent to the British king, George III, to explain why Americans were going to fight him for their freedom.

The Declaration of Independence was approved on July 4, 1776, the first Independence Day. That is why we call the Fourth of July our nation's birthday.

Happy 4ᵗʰ of July!

American flags, fireworks, and parades all help us celebrate and honor our country.

## Abraham Lincoln

Abraham Lincoln is the third Mount Rushmore president. He was born in Kentucky in a small house made of logs. This log cabin had only one room, one window, and a dirt floor. Abraham's father made him a bed from logs and dried corn leaves.

Later, Abraham lived in Indiana. There were very few stores where the Lincolns lived. The family had to grow their own food. The Lincolns had to make almost everything they needed. They chopped down trees for firewood. They made their table and chairs and spoons out of wood.

Abraham was often called Abe. Abe learned how to read and write. He made a pen from a turkey feather and used berry juice for ink. Abe had few books of his own, but his family had a Bible. Abe read it over and over. Abe taught himself many things by reading.

Once, Abe borrowed a book from a neighbor. At home, he stored it between the logs of the cabin near his bed. But water came through the logs and soaked the book. Abe was sad. He went to his neighbor and told him what had happened. The neighbor asked Abe to do some chores for him, and then he gave the book to Abe. The book was *The Life of George Washington*.

As a young man, Abe lived in Illinois. He was strong and tall and had many different jobs. Abe worked as a log splitter and as a farmworker. He became a clerk in a store. Once, he walked a long way to give back a few pennies to someone who had paid too much. He became known as Honest Abe.

Abe really wanted to be a lawyer. He studied hard to become one. He worked for the Illinois government and helped to write state laws.

Abe did so well in the government of Illinois that his friends told him to run for president. Abraham Lincoln became the sixteenth president, during a difficult time in our history.

# Theodore Roosevelt

Theodore Roosevelt was sick a lot when he was a boy. So, Theodore hardly ever went to school. Instead, teachers came to his home to teach him. That sounds pretty lonely, doesn't it? However, Theodore said he was a very happy child. Theodore was often called Teddy.

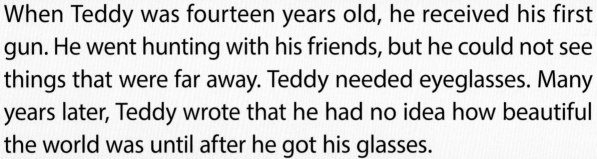

When Teddy was fourteen years old, he received his first gun. He went hunting with his friends, but he could not see things that were far away. Teddy needed eyeglasses. Many years later, Teddy wrote that he had no idea how beautiful the world was until after he got his glasses.

Although he had been sick as a young boy, Teddy exercised and grew up to become a strong man who loved being outdoors. He started working in the government in New York. A few years later, he bought two ranches out west. He wore cowboy clothes and rode horses to round up his cattle. He hunted bison.

Teddy went back to New York City and became the head of the police force. Then Spain and the United States went to war against each other. Teddy Roosevelt joined the army. He was the leader of a group of soldiers called the Rough Riders.

Teddy Roosevelt came to see how important the land is to all living things. Once he took a trip into the mountains. There he saw forests filled with plants and animals. He worried that someday they would all be gone.

When Teddy Roosevelt became the twenty-sixth president, he made new rules for areas of forest in America. On this special land, people could not harm trees or animals.

**Core Knowledge**®

# CKHG™

## Core Knowledge HISTORY AND GEOGRAPHY™

**Editorial Directors**

Linda Bevilacqua and Rosie McCormick

## Subject Matter Expert

J. Chris Arndt, PhD, Department of History, James Madison University

## Illustration and Photo Credits

3LH / SuperStock: 5d

Abraham Lincoln rides into Gettysburg (colour litho), McBride, Angus (1931-2007) / Private Collection / © Look and Learn / Bridgeman Images: i, iii, 24

Buddy Mays / Alamy Stock Photo: 15c

Charles O. Cecil / Alamy Stock Photo: 13a

College of William and Mary in 1839, 1920 (lithograph), American School, (20th century) / Private Collection / Photo © GraphicaArtis / Bridgeman Images: 14a

Crossing the Delaware River on Christmas Night, McConnell, James Edwin (1903-95) / Private Collection / © Look and Learn / Bridgeman Images: 11b

Delphotos / Alamy Stock Photo: 17a

Dennis Cox / Alamy Stock Photo: 15b

George Washington being sworn in as the first President of America in New York (gouache on paper), English School, (20th century) / Private Collection / © Look and Learn / Bridgeman Images: 12

George Washington, having cut down the cherry tree, with his father (gouache on paper), Jackson, Peter (1922-2003) / Private Collection / © Look and Learn / Bridgeman Images: 8

Heritage Image Partnership Ltd / Alamy Stock Photo: 16b

Hum Images / Alamy Stock Photo: 7a

Ivy Close Images / Alamy Stock Photo: 22

Jakub Gojda / Alamy Stock Photo: 13b

Kevin Shields / Alamy Stock Photo: 18

mark reinstein / Alamy Stock Photo: 7b

nagelestock.com / Alamy Stock Photo: Cover D, 2

North Wind Picture Archives / Alamy Stock Photo: 20, 23, 29

Officer of the 23rd Regiment of Foot Royal Welsh Fuzileers 1775, 2005 (oil on canvas), Troiani, Don (b.1949) / Private Collection / Bridgeman Images: 11a

Portrait of George Washington taking the Salute at Trenton, (oil on canvas), Faed, John (1820-1902) / Private Collection / Photo © Christie's Images / Bridgeman Images: Cover B, 5a

Portrait of Thomas Jefferson, 1786 (oil on canvas), Brown, Mather (1761-1831) / National Portrait Gallery, Washington DC, USA / Photo © GraphicaArtis / Bridgeman Images: Cover C, 14b

Robert Wyatt / Alamy Stock Photo: 6

roberto galan / Alamy Stock Photo: 17b

Science History Images / Alamy Stock Photo: Cover A, 3a, 3b

Tetra Images / SuperStock: 4b

The Home of George Washington, Mount Vernon, Virginia, published by Nathaniel Currier (1813-88) and James Merritt Ives (1824-95) (colour litho), American School, (19th century) / Yale University Art Gallery, New Haven, CT, USA / Bridgeman Images: 10

Theodore Roosevelt leading the 'Rough Riders' during the Spanish-American War, detail of a painting by W.G. Road, 1898 (colour litho), American School, (19th century) / Private Collection / Peter Newark American Pictures / Bridgeman Images: 28

Thomas Jefferson with his servants and slaves in constructing Monticello (colour litho), Meltzoff, Stanley (1917-2006) / National Geographic Creative / Silverfish Press/National Geographic Image Collection / Bridgeman Images: 15a

Thomas Jefferson Writing the Declaration of Independence, from 'The Story of the Revolution' by Henry Cabot Lodge (1850-1924), published in Scribner's Magazine, March 1898 (oil on canvas), Pyle, Howard (1853-1911) / Delaware Art Museum, Wilmington, USA / Howard Pyle Collection / Bridgeman Images: 5b

Thomas Jefferson writing, 2007 (w/c on paper), Wood, Rob (b.1946) / Private Collection / Wood Ronsaville Harlin, Inc. USA / Bridgeman Images: 16a

When They Were Young: Abraham Lincoln, Jackson, Peter (1922-2003) / Private Collection / © Look and Learn / Bridgeman Images: 5c

World History Archive / Alamy Stock Photo: 4a

Young Washington, Surveyor, North American, (19th century) / Private Collection / © Look and Learn / Bridgeman Images: 9